CALLED TO LEAD

CALLED TO LEAD

52 WEEKLY DEVOTIONS FOR WORKPLACE LEADERS

WRITTEN BY JOHN CROSBY

AMBASSADOR INTERNATIONAL
GREENVILLE, SOUTH CAROLINA & BELFAST, NORTHERN IRELAND

www.ambassador-international.com

Called to Lead
52 Weekly Devotions for Workplace Leaders

Printed in the United States of America

ISBN: 978-1-62020-021-6
eISBN: 978-1-62020-022-3

Cover Design by Matthew Mulder
Page Layout by Kelley Moore of Points & Picas

AMBASSADOR INTERNATIONAL
Emerald House
427 Wade Hampton Blvd.
Greenville, SC 29609, USA
www.ambassador-international.com

AMBASSADOR BOOKS
The Mount
2 Woodstock Link
Belfast, BT6 8DD, Northern Ireland, UK
www.ambassador-international.com

The colophon is a trademark of Ambassador

Called to Lead is dedicated to the workplace leaders who
have trusted me to serve them and learn from
them through the ministry of Priority Insight for the last
twelve years. Without these faithful, trusting, sometimes
trying men and women, I may have missed many of the
principles shared in this book.

Called to Lead is also dedicated to my family,
Jo, Erin, Wesley, and Jeff. Your love, patience, respect,
encouragement, successes and trials have taught me rich
lessons about life, faith, and leadership. My most
important leadership role is serving you.

Thank you.

Endorsements

"Ignore the thick heavy books. Pick up this treasure chest of wisdom with hundreds of priceless nuggets on practical biblical leadership. John Crosby has hit a home run with 52 weekly singles that we can chew on one small bite at a time."

Kent Humphreys, Ambassador FCCI/
Christ@Work, Author

Every Christian must grow in their knowledge and maturity to reflect Christ's nature. John Crosby's *Called to Lead* provides daily encouragement that every leader will benefit. Each message provides food for the soul for those who desire to be God's leader.

Os Hillman, author, *TGIF Today God
Is First* and *Change Agent*

Called to Lead is short, to the point, and worth reading. John Crosby addresses practical biblical challenges that real leaders face week in and week out in the workplace. This book will help anyone discern God's perspective and align their leadership decisions with Him.

Dr. Mark Cress, *Founder / CEO
Corporate Chaplains of America, Inc*

"Be ready to experience the word of God in this unique devotional . . . specifically designed for those involved in leading others. John Crosby was inspired to create "Called to Lead . . . a powerful tool to help you get your week started with practical tools that you can apply to your life as a leader.

Jim Smith, Business Leader & Friend

John Crosby left a promising future with an established family business to join the ministry. His business success provides him a unique perspective that allows him to teach and apply biblical principles to everyday workplace situations. Every business leader could benefit greatly from his teachings.

Walter Lewis, Business Leader & Friend

"With God's blessings, I had the opportunity to rise to the very top of the Georgia State Senate as President Pro Tempore and, ultimately, to be a candidate for Governor. I have read dozens of leadership books throughout my career in politics, but only a few reinforced the critical skill sets needed with scripture. True leadership must be modeled on the brief, but powerful, example offered by Jesus Christ and based on the Word of God. Called to Lead by John Crosby should be on the desk of every leader who seeks to effectively serve his or her spiritual calling with wisdom and humbleness."

May God bless this effort!

Eric Johnson, FAIA President

I have known John Crosby since the day he gave his life to Christ. Since then he has made a life-changing impact for Christ because of his commitment to ministering to people in the business sector of our community. I'm sure as you read this book his insight will impact you as well.

Cam Huxford, Pastor, Savannah Christian Church

CONTENTS

CALLED TO...

Leadership is first and foremost a calling. God chose you to lead and has entrusted you with opportunities, resources, and relationships. Your primary responsibility as a leader is to wisely steward that which God has entrusted to you. The Called To series is intended to assist you in developing this wise stewardship by providing specific groups of leaders with biblical insight into specific leadership arenas and challenging you to align your lives and leadership with God's Word.

Each book in the *Called To* series is written in a weekly devotional format intended to give the reader:

- one biblical principle or challenge
- the time to pray and perhaps discuss the principle

- the opportunity to focus on that principle for a week, trusting God to provide opportunities to see that principle at work within the week

In my ministry serving leaders, this combination of reading, praying, discussing, and seeking to discern one principle each week throughout the year has proven to be an effective approach to developing wise leaders. I trust you will find this series to be an effective tool in your pursuit of honoring the God who called you to lead.

Lead wisely,
John Crosby

INTRODUCTION

As I write this introduction, I am finding myself moved by the twelve years of laughter, tears, prayers, victories, and losses that have forged the writing of these devotions. Since 2000, I have been daily coaching, teaching, encouraging, and challenging workplace leaders in their calling to honor God through their leadership. Each of these devotions has been forged, tested, and found true through the individual lives of leaders I have served. Some of these devotions stem from great kingdom victories and personal growth. Others were written in hopes that painful failures might not be repeated.

The workplace leaders whom I serve tend to be smart, hard-working, no-nonsense leaders. They are not looking for someone to warm their hearts or cram more Scripture between their ears. They are looking for something solid that will help them become better leaders. They have an understanding that leadership is a calling and that the Bible is the greatest source of leadership principles the world has ever known, even if they do not know where to find those principles. These workplace leaders are looking for help in closing the gap between the leaders they are and the leaders God created them to be. If you resonate with this description, *Called to Lead* was written for you.

This book is not intended to be read in a few quick sittings, or even to be read daily. These devotions are intended to be read weekly, followed by a prayer asking God to reveal this principle at work in the following week. It is not meant to replace any daily reading, study, or prayer to which you have already committed. It is meant to challenge you to consider a biblical leadership principle and simply chew on it for a week, trusting the Holy Spirit to help you wisely steward the leadership that God has entrusted to you.

So grab a cup of coffee or OJ, sit back in your favorite chair, and start your week by investing a few minutes pondering the intersection of God's Word and your life and leadership. I'm confident you'll be glad you did.

Lead wisely,

John Crosby

TRUST

*Jesus answered, "I am the way and **the truth** and the life."*

John 14:6

Trust is the most fundamental leadership need. With it, a leader can overcome many obstacles and shortcomings. Without trust, little else matters. Throughout the New Testament, Jesus began his teaching by saying *I tell you the truth*. The Gospel of John gave Jesus' purpose as coming to testify to *the truth*. Jesus actually claimed to be *the Truth*. The Holy Spirit was introduced and described by Jesus as the *Spirit of Truth*. On the other hand, Satan is commonly referred to as *the father of lies* and *the Deceiver*.

The surest way to be a trusted leader begins with knowing and following the One who is described within the

Word of God as *the Truth*. Building trust means first knowing truth and being trustworthy, then investing enough time into relationships that people see the real you. This is clear, simple, and undeniable. Yet it's not what most leaders want to hear. We'd much rather seek shortcuts. Americans in particular spend countless hours and resources on trust-building exercises, excursions, discussions, and trainings, most often with little to no long-term benefit.

Gallup's research on teams found that the most successful teams talked very little about trust, while the topic of trust dominated the conversations of struggling teams. Why? Because *building trust is not a competence. Building relationships is.* Trust, respect, integrity, and honesty are developed and revealed through strong relationships.

Newsflash: *Encouraging relationships flat-out trumps competence in building trust.*

- So what does this tell us about our approach to team-building?
- Are we building relationships or fruitlessly attempting to build trust?
- How do we develop a culture of trust within our team?

GAINING WISDOM

If any of you lacks wisdom, he should ask God, who gives generously to all without finding fault, and it will be given to him.

James 1:5

When the Bible speaks of wisdom, it is referring to God's perspective. To gain wisdom is to gain God's perspective. I love the sarcasm in James' writing: *If any of you lacks wisdom…* Clearly, we each lack wisdom. Proverbs 1:7 says *Fear of the Lord is the beginning of wisdom.* Each passage is pointing to humility as the beginning of wisdom. James says I must first acknowledge that I lack wisdom before I can gain wisdom. I must acknowledge that I don't have all the answers, that I don't even have all the questions. Fear of the Lord is that recognition that there is a God, and I am not him.

The great news in the verse above is that when I real-ize I need God's perspective on my job, my spouse, my life, my circumstances... I simply need to ask, not for God to fill my prescription for solving my problems, but for him to show me his perspective. There are no hoops, no mantras, no minimal requirements, because God knows when we see the gap between our lives and his will, wisdom always brings its own conviction.

Do you have the humility and courage to ask God to re-veal his perspective on the most troubling areas of your life?

LIVING WATER

On the last and greatest day of the Feast, Jesus stood and said in a loud voice, "If anyone is thirsty, let him come to me and drink. Whoever believes in me, as the Scripture has said, streams of living water will flow from within him." By this he meant the Spirit, whom those who believed in him were later to receive.

John 7:37-39

Water, especially drinking water, is one of our planet's most valuable resources. Throughout history, man has developed communities around sources of drinking water. Access to clean drinking water has clearly proven to be an essential element of any sustainable community. Whole communities have been lost as a result of losing their supply of drinking water.

If the sustainability of a community is at risk when access to drinking water is limited, how much is at risk when Christian leaders fail to share living water within our organizations? We have been entrusted with shaping the character and influencing the future of the people we lead. God entrusted us with team members and opportunities, and he empowered us with his Spirit. When we spend time in his Word and in prayer, he refreshes and rehydrates us, preparing us for anything our opposition can offer. He says above that "living water will flow from us." When we lose interest in him and make excuses, we compromise his trust and offer unsteady, unclear, weak, and often selfish leadership. If you take your calling to lead seriously, make it a point never to address your team members before getting refreshed and rehydrated.

IRON SHARPENS IRON

As iron sharpens iron, so one man sharpens another.

Proverbs 27:17

Everyone wants to succeed, but few people structure for success. We want the benefits without the work, rewards without challenges, and recognition before projects are completed. Solomon gives us a crucial element of success in this verse. It is a focused, Christ-centered relationship with a peer.

You could put a workplace leader, a preacher, and a coach in an accountability group, and each could consistently make excuses for falling short of expectations by suggesting that the others did not understand the demands of his life. However, put two or three workplace leaders—who see each other as equals, trust one another, understand each other's work, and perhaps know each others' spouse and children—together in an accountability group, and it opens a whole new world of transparency, accountability, support, affirmation, correction, and friendship. According to Solomon, a peer who is willing to open God's Word with you to give and receive advice, counsel, and correction is one of the best prescriptions for success.

Perhaps it's time to find another workplace leader to join you in an *iron sharpening iron* relationship.

THE BIG KAHUNA

Reckless words pierce like a sword, but the tongue of the wise brings healing.

Proverbs 12:18

Take a minute and reflect on your life. Which leader had the greatest influence on your life? I'm betting the "Big Kahuna" was not necessarily the most educated or wealthiest leader you knew. He (or she) was a leader who weighed his words wisely. He understood that criticism, cynicism, and sarcasm weigh much more than words of affirmation, encouragement, and insight. He saw potential in you and sought to bring it out, using accountability to build you up rather than tear you down.

Leadership matters, and the words of a leader carry tremendous weight. Wise leaders weigh their words wisely.

Now, you're the Big Kahuna in someone else's eyes. You have been entrusted with people to lead and opportunities to build those people up. What the Big Kahuna says carries tremendous weight in the lives of your team members. You have the power to build up, to heal, to tear down, and to pierce. Weigh your words wisely, leaving your team walking taller than when you arrived.

AND THEN SOME

Suppose one of you had a servant plowing or looking after the sheep. Would he say to the servant when he comes in from the field, "Come along now and sit down to eat"? Would he not rather say, "Prepare my supper, get yourself ready and wait on me while I eat and drink; after that you may eat and drink"? Would he thank the servant because he did what he was told to do? So you also, when you have done everything you were told to do, should say, "We are unworthy servants; we have only done our duty."

Luke 17:7-10

Few people would consider doing only what is required as a character flaw, but the Bible says otherwise. Most people fall into one of two categories: Those who *do just enough* and those who complete what is required *and then some*. The first group does *just enough* to get by, *just enough* to get paid, *just enough* to avoid getting fired. The second group is not necessarily smarter or more talented, but they consistently exceed expectations—outworking, outthinking, and outsmarting others—simply doing what others are unwilling to do, say, learn, or risk. According to Jesus, if we do only what we are required to do, our performance is nothing special and is unworthy of reward. If you want to build a team that goes "the extra mile," it starts with modeling an *and then some* attitude.

DO YOU CARE ABOUT ME?

...love your neighbor as yourself.

Matthew 22:39

It may be cliché, but people still want to know how much you care before they care how much you know. Most leaders have never had a course on compassion, but it is a crucial component to any long-term leadership success. Compassion is simply the act of putting another's needs ahead of one's own. At the very root of compassion is grace, the recognition that we have received so much more than we deserve. I'm uncertain how anyone can be consistently compassionate without recognition of grace resonating deep inside. I'm just as uncertain as to how someone who claims to grasp grace could live a life lacking compassion. Grace transcends human logic and brings the spiritual into play in our everyday lives. It opens the portal for seeing, feeling, and experiencing the life-changing love of God. When this grace is worked out through people, it's called compassion.

Nothing works better in the short term than intimidating people and coercing them to do exactly what you want. Your team will jump to attention every time you come into a room and agree with everything you say. Perhaps you've chosen to ignore your reputation, your future, your credibility, or the loyalty of the people around you. Just bark orders and hope for the best. This is the playbook of the schoolyard bully.

Over the long term, however, things are different. People need to know you care about them before they will follow you long term. Leaders who adhere to the fear-based model of leadership often become former leaders lamenting the "betrayal" of their people in their "times of greatest need."

40 WAYS TO MOVE 40 MEN

*There are different kinds of gifts, but the same spirit.
There are different kinds of service, but the same Lord.
There are different kinds of working, but the same God
works all of them in all men.*

1 Corinthians 12:4-6

Vince Lombardi, the legendary coach of the Green Bay Packers, never had a losing season. After assuming his first professional head coaching position with a team that had gone 1-10-1 the previous season, he coached 146 games, winning 105, losing 35, tying 6, and earning a 9-1 postseason record. He achieved this record before the advent of free agency, playing only with the players he had and leading thirteen players from the 1-10-1 team to become All Pros for the Packers.

When asked about the secret of his success, Lombardi was fond of saying, "My job is to find forty different ways to move forty different men." In other words, he went to great lengths to treat every player as a unique individual. Lombardi knew that Bart Starr hated being yelled at in public, so he confronted Starr only in private. On the other hand, he knew that Lee Roy Caffey responded better to harsh, public confrontation, and Lombardi was happy to oblige. His star receiver, Max McGee, hated blocking drills, so he rewarded McGee's game-time blocks by giving him alternative drills during practice.

Assembly-line leadership styles that treat every team member like another head in a herd of cattle leave much talent and opportunity unrealized. Your team members are individuals. Do you know them well enough to know what moves each of them? Why not? Could finding the different ways to move each team member be the secret to your success?

STRONG, ENDURING TEAMS

If a house is divided against itself, that house cannot stand.

Mark 3:25

Is there anything worse than attempting a project with a team that is strangled by dissension? It chokes any sense of accomplishment right out of a team. There is no substitute for unity. It is absolutely essential for any sustainable success.

The key word is "sustainable." Are you simply looking to get through the pending deadline or current firestorm? Or are you seeking to build an enduring team? A good manager can manage the ins and outs of a fragmented team to achieve short-term success. But it takes a leader with the appropriate skills and courage to overcome dissension and build an enduring team.

Unity is not about eliminating conflict. Indeed, every strong, enduring team is comprised of members with different strengths and perspectives. When differences are focused on issues and are addressed openly, clearly, and respectfully among the team, they often bring the strongest resolutions. Yet, when members turn the conflicts into quarrels by making them personal, a wise leader knows his "house is divided against itself," and his team must be addressed.

CUTTING CORNERS

Stolen water is sweet; food eaten in secret is delicious! But little do they know that the dead are there, that her guests are in the depths of the grave.

Proverbs 9:17-18

Regardless of your work, there is always a way to bend the rules or cut corners, and there is always someone who thinks he can get away with it. Whether it's exaggerating product claims, "taking care" of an illegal offense, "fudging" a report, or substituting a lower grade material, cutting corners is wrong; the Bible says that those who are seduced by the temptation to cut corners will pay a heavy price.

If you succeed at cutting corners without others realizing what you have done, you will find the rewards hollow and unfulfilling, even while others acknowledge your achievement. But the price goes beyond lack of fulfillment. The Bible says that secretly gaining what you do not deserve leads to death. How much pride does it take to know that the God who spoke the world into existence, the Alpha and the Omega, and the One who bore our sins and was nailed to a tree for our salvation says cutting corners will kill you, and you keep cutting corners? If you or those you have been entrusted to lead are "bending the rules," stop.

CALLED TO LEAD

Brothers, I do not consider myself yet to have taken hold of it. But one thing I do: Forgetting what is behind and straining toward what is ahead, I press on toward the goal to win the prize for which God has called me heavenward in Christ Jesus.

Philippians 3:13-14

What happens when a leader mistakes one big success for a successful career? When we assume that one success will propel us to future success, we often fail to adequately prepare for the opportunities and challenges before us. Great victories bring more focused opposition, which requires more focused preparation. Also, God tends to reward success with bigger challenges.

When a Christian leader relies on the stories, testimonies, and lessons from his past to prepare him for the opportunities before him, he often finds himself lacking the wisdom and influence needed to help those he has been entrusted to lead. The Apostle Paul never got so enamored with one success that he forgot to prepare for the next challenge. His example is to avoid resting on the successes of yesterday and to strain forward, preparing for what is ahead. Are you serious about being called to lead? Are you pressing forward in your desire to honor God? Are you spending enough time in Scripture and prayer to prepare for whatever lies ahead?

FIRST FORGIVE

> *Therefore, if you are offering your gift at the altar and there remember that your brother has something against you, leave your gift there in front of the altar. First go and be reconciled to your brother, then come and offer your gift.*

Matthew 5:23-24

For most of the leaders I serve, this is the most significant character flaw I see. Leaders tend to be competitive. Yet competitive people tend to hold grudges. We begrudge former staff for leaving our organization; we resent competitors who seek to sway our customers, and family members who don't support or appreciate our sacrifices; we stay ticked about costly in-house mistakes; we get peeved when a friend supports our competition. Some of these issues we attempt to reconcile, and some we just think we'll take to the grave.

Few things have the potential to undermine and thwart a leader's attempt to positively influence others like a bitter heart.

STOP. *If you're breaking down the above passage and pointing out that if the other person does not know about your anger then he can't hold it against you...* just stop. You're missing the point! Anger is like weed seeds. Spread a few in your yard and see what happens. When anger takes root, sin takes hold. Anger will choke the joy right out of your life. God values your obedience FAR MORE than your worship and/or ministry activity. That's why he says stop and reconcile BEFORE worshipping.

Perhaps you need to put this devotion down right now, swallow your pride, and make a tough phone call or–even better–*man-up (or woman-up)* and go reconcile with someone in person. I'm pleading with you.

If someone has come to mind while reading this, don't try to determine *if* you should address the situation. Trust the Holy Spirit and take care of business. I know of nothing more personally freeing and blessed more often by God than when we extend forgiveness and reconcile with others. I can promise you this–when you truly forgive the person you least wish to forgive, your load will be lightened more than you expect. It always is when we follow Christ. Indeed, what could be more Christ-like than going the extra mile and extending forgiveness, even to someone who may not deserve your forgiveness?

PRIDE AND KUDZU

Pride goes before destruction, a haughty spirit before a fall.

Proverbs 16:18

Have you ever noticed the difference between what the world says it expects and how it reacts when those expectations bear fruit? Lately I have been noticing how many schools and businesses have *P R I D E* painted boldly on their walls. Dozens of teams have *P R I D E* printed on shirts and jackets. Parking lots reserve the spaces closest to the building for those with the most authority or those being recognized for "being the best."

The irony is that while we're busy instilling *P R I D E* in our people, nothing is quite as distasteful as the selfish, arrogant actions that result from our teaching. We want our teams to be proud of themselves and our organization, yet we are repulsed by conceited, ostentatious interactions with others. It's like planting kudzu and expecting it to bear oranges. Not only will kudzu fail to bear oranges, it is nearly impossible to contain.

P R I D E and kudzu are similar in that they eventually take over everything around them.

In recent weeks, I have had two people point out selfish, prideful acts of two different leaders involved in our ministry. I don't think either leader was intentional in the way he was treating others. Yet it would be hard not to perceive the actions of either as self-centered. That's the point. We don't need to teach *P R I D E*. It comes naturally. Since selfish pride is part of our natural state of fallenness, we should be intentional about humility. If we want orange juice, we should plant oranges rather than kudzu. We should be teaching and modeling humility if we want better functioning, highly successful teams. The world may be yelling and cheering for more pride, but in the end it will reject the "fruit" of its own sowing.

PASSION AND PURPOSE

Folly delights a man who lacks judgment, but a man of understanding keeps a straight course.

Proverbs 15:21

Would you seriously consider hiring someone to pastor your church who just needed a job and had no particular passion or purpose? Why or why not? What happens when someone accepts a leadership position simply because no one else will or because he needs the money?

Godly people recognize leadership as a calling. They recognize that God has entrusted them with opportunities to lead and he expects them to wisely steward everything he entrusts to them. Leadership is a calling which should never be taken lightly.

Leaders who lack passion and purpose are easily distracted. Passion and purpose keep the leader and those he has been entrusted to lead away from "folly" and on a "straight course." Are your passion and purpose clear? Do others align themselves easily with your direction? If not, perhaps it is time to quietly and intentionally rethink your direction, asking God for his direction.

YOUR INNER CIRCLE

My soul is overwhelmed with sorrow to the point of death. Stay here and keep watch with me.

Matthew 26:38

Pause a minute and think about the words above. Jesus, the Alpha and the Omega, was asking his friends to help him with an emotional struggle. It's amazing to me that the greatest leader of all time would show such vulnerability.

A leader who keeps everyone at arm's length never optimizes his potential. No matter how important and high profile we become, we need an inner circle of friends whom we can call upon in emotional struggles. I have often watched strong, talented leaders leave an organization short of their goals largely because they never really developed close relationships with the people around them.

Jesus concentrated much of his energy on befriending and developing a small inner circle of people he led. He knew that when his inner circle gained his insight and inspiration, it would exponentially increase his impact. This kind of reaching influence is seldom achieved through staff meetings and simply working together. Jesus shared life with his inner circle. He served them and called upon them for help.

Naturally, many leaders will choose the tough, emotionless, Spartan persona with their peers because that's what they have been taught. But really, do you get any tougher than allowing yourself to be mocked, beaten, and nailed to a tree to save others? Perhaps it's time to study a new "tough guy" for leadership and friendship.

THE INVITATION OF SATAN

The lips of the righteous know what is fitting, but the mouth of the wicked only what is perverse.

Proverbs 10:32

If anyone considers himself religious and yet does not keep a tight rein on his tongue, he deceives himself, and his religion is worthless.

James 1:26

Ever notice how some people just fall into the habit of cursing in practically any and all circumstances? Leaders who profess their faith and seek to be godly leaders may begin using profanity to make a point, and before long, they are using increasingly strong language in everyday talk and finding it "necessary" to be more perverse when attempting to make an impact.

The Bible says that our language is indicative of the condition of our heart. We can kid ourselves about the two being unrelated. We can justify our language by comparing it to those around us. Certainly there are few words which will shock many in today's workplaces. Yet, that's the invitation of Satan. He loves it when we compare ourselves to anyone other than Christ. Doing so inevitably keeps us from noticing the gradual decline of our passion and commitment to Jesus. Foolish words are just the beginning of that slippery slope.

If you believe in the lordship of Jesus Christ, the sacrificial atonement he made for your sins, and his omnipresence (seeing and hearing everything we do), ask yourself if you would speak the same words if you could see him standing next to you.

GRASSHOPPERS IN OUR OWN EYES

The land we explored devoured those living in it. All the people we saw there are of great size... We seemed like grasshoppers in our own eyes, and we looked the same to them.

Numbers 13:32-33

You've seen it. You work hard to prepare your team. You have succeeded at increasingly complex challenges. Then the big opportunity arrives, a project the size of which you have only dreamed. The eyes of your team members are as big as saucers. They are overwhelmed. Perhaps it's the budget. Maybe it's the visibility, or just the sheer size of the client. But deep down, you know—your team members are grasshoppers in their own eyes. The size of the potential obstacles has thwarted them before they even started.

For vast numbers of Americans, life has become staggeringly easy–and incredibly unfulfilling. We have empowered people to perfect the art of avoiding any real challenge. Life in modern society is designed to eliminate as many unforeseen events as possible, and as inviting as that seems, it leaves people hopelessly unfulfilled, bored, and destined for a rude awakening in their significant personal and professional challenges. If we allow shallow excuses rather than heightened performances when facing overwhelming odds, we destine our team members to lives of mediocrity.

As leaders, we must recognize the magnitude of what we have been entrusted to do. The workplace pits men and women in situations where the outcome is not entirely within their control. We prepare and equip them for life's challenges when we influence them to perform at their best even when they are out-sized, out-manned, and just inexperienced. Courage is not the absence of fear, but the discipline to perform in the face of fear. Are you developing courage or making excuses?

FROM LION TO LOAF

For these commands are a lamp, this teaching is a light, and the corrections of discipline are the way to life, keeping you from the immoral woman, from the smooth tongue of the wayward wife. Do not lust in your heart after her beauty or let her captivate you with her eyes, for the prostitute reduces you to a loaf of bread, and the adulteress preys upon your very life.

Proverbs 6:23-26

Most leaders are like lions. They want to rule their domain. They are bold, courageous, and forward thinking. No one need go before them. They will blaze their own trails and write their own stories. They earn and expect respect. Their fears are few and rarely revealed. A good leader is seldom distracted from a well-prepared plan. But the beauty, smooth tongue, and captivating eyes of a wayward wife have reduced many to a loaf of bread.

Don't fool yourself. It's not a matter of if you have this weakness, but of how you prepare for it. Be on guard. If you are more relaxed or casual about honoring and protecting your marriage than you are about executing your business plan, you're headed for the oven.

WORTH YOUR SALT

You are the salt of the earth. But if the salt loses its saltiness, how can it be made salty again? It is no longer good for anything, except to be thrown out and trampled by men.

Matthew 5:13

I love wrestling. In fact, anyone who spends significant time with me hears about weight classes, tournaments, brackets, pins, camps... I don't try to recruit my friends to wrestle. I don't seek to teach them wrestling moves. I don't even plan to talk about wrestling. It just comes out. I'm passionate about wrestling, and it just comes out in conversations in every area of my life. I don't even have to initiate wrestling conversations. Once people know my passion, it is the most natural thing in the world for them to ask me about my passion. I'm guessing you're just as passionate about something, and that passion seasons many of your conversations.

That's exactly what Jesus meant when he said that we are the salt of the earth. Our love for him and our gratitude for what he did should season every area of our lives. You may not be called to preach or even teach the gospel. But you have been given an extraordinary gift, and you are expected to be passionately grateful. When we love the Lord our God with all our heart, all our soul, and all our mind (The Greatest Commandment, Matthew 22:37), that passion comes out in every area of our lives. People who know us know our passions. We don't have to preach, teach, judge, or "evangelize." When our passion is clear, people will ask about it.

How often do people ask about your passion? When is the last time that someone outside your church asked you about Jesus?

THE CHINESE BAMBOO TREE

Brothers, I could not address you as spiritual but as worldly—mere infants in Christ. I gave you milk, not solid food, for you were not yet ready for it. Indeed, you are still not ready. You are still worldly. For since there is jealousy and quarreling among you, are you not worldly?

1 Corinthians 3:1-3

Can you identify with Paul? Have you poured yourself into your team, only to find them arguing, fighting, acting immaturely? Take heart. Even the Apostle Paul experienced great struggles while seeking to develop people.

If you were called to lead, you have been entrusted to develop people. Some people will show signs of growth early. Others may not seem to be growing at all. Consider the Chinese bamboo tree. This remarkable tree shows no outward signs of growth until its fifth year. You plant the bulb and water a small shoot for four years while seeing absolutely no growth. However, growth is taking place. This tiny tree spends four years developing an enormous network of underground roots. In fact, your strongest team members would find it nearly impossible to yank, jerk, twist, or tug this tiny four-year-old tree out of the ground. Then, in its fifth year, this tiny tree with an enormous root system erupts into a staggering height of eighty feet.

Keep planting and watering. You have no idea what God is doing below the surface. Trust him to provide the growth. He may not choose to work on our timetable, but he always uses what we make available.

BREAK ROOM FIRES

The tongue is a small part of the body, but it makes great boasts. Consider what a great forest is set on fire by a small spark. The tongue also is a fire, a world of evil among the parts of the body. It corrupts the whole person, sets the whole course of life on fire, and is itself set on fire by hell.

James 3:5-6

Depending on your workplace, you probably have certain injuries that are somewhat commonplace. However, without knowing your business, I can tell you the most injury-prone body part in your workplace. It is the tongue, not because it gets injured, but because it habitually inflicts injury.

If you had team members lighting fires in the break room, you would be foolish not to address them. Yet I have seen leaders ignore much more dangerous "loose tongues" on their teams. Make no mistake, nothing has more potential to undermine leadership, destroy team unity, crush hopeful aspirations, and shape your team's future than words. The more well-known you become, the more you will have to hear and ignore the poisonous comments of those outside your leadership influence. But a wise leader uses his influence to extinguish the fires in his own break room.

FOLLOW WHOLEHEARTEDLY

But my brothers who went up with me made the hearts of the people melt with fear. I, however, followed the Lord my God wholeheartedly. So on that day Moses swore to me, "The land on which your feet have walked will be your inheritance and that of your children forever, because you have followed the Lord my God wholeheartedly."

Joshua 14:8-9

Caleb was an extraordinary leader. He was one of the twelve spies Moses sent into the Promised Land. His report was full of anticipation and confidence. He was ready to take the land. But he was out-voted ten to two. He stood his ground and nobly argued what he correctly discerned was God's calling. Yet, fear led the people to reject his desire to take the land. The price of their fear was severe—forty years wandering in the desert.

Caleb adjusted his course, suffering alongside those he was entrusted to lead. But he never abandoned his passion or his purpose. Nearly forty-five years later, at age eighty-five, Caleb was rewarded with the very land he wished to take from the "giants" who caused so much fear.

Passion and purpose are transcendent. Caleb found both in following the Lord wholeheartedly. Leaders who do so have far more growth, enthusiasm, and unity than others. Employees and customers eagerly transfer to join their organizations. But it can't be faked, and it does not come without costs. Will you follow God wholeheartedly when others shy away? God always rewards the kind of wholehearted, patient, steadfast purpose and passion demonstrated by Caleb.

KEEPING YOUR OATH

He who keeps his oath even when it hurts... will never be shaken.

Psalms 15:4b

Be honest. When is the last time you made a casual commitment that you never intended to keep?

"I'll call you later."

"I'll look into that."

"We'll do so next time."

Is it possible that your word meant a lot more to someone else than it did to you? Or perhaps you made a commitment that you fully intended to keep, but "things changed." It's interesting what kinds of things we can find more valuable than our word: convenience, acceptance, pride, finances...

"Keeping your oath even when it hurts" means that you'll do *what* you said you'll do, *when* you said you'd do it, and *how* you said you'd do it, even if it becomes more costly, inconvenient, or time-consuming than you planned. A friend of mine, whose grandfather was sheriff of a nearby county for many years, said his grandfather taught him to make as few promises as possible and to keep every one. That's good advice.

TIME THIEVES

Moses' father-in-law replied, "What you are doing is not good. You and these people who come to you will only wear yourselves out. The work is too heavy for you; you cannot handle it alone."

Exodus 18:17-18

E very leader understands the need to prioritize responsibilities. But what do you do next? What do you do after you have identified what matters most?

The next step is to identify what you must stop doing in order to do what matters most. Time is your only irreplaceable asset. When an hour or a day is gone, it is gone. We each have less time ahead of us now than we had last week. This makes identifying the things that interfere with us doing what matters most absolutely critical. Before you begin adding tasks to an already blossoming "to-do" list, most of us need to create a "stop- doing" list. We need to identify the convenient, tough, urgent, easy, enjoyable, fearful, or prideful issues that steal our time and keep us from accomplishing what matters most. Our unidentified time thieves are robbing us blind!

In Exodus 18:13-26, we're told that Moses sat "from morning till evening" as he attempted to settle each of the disputes among his two million followers. His father-in-law, Jethro, saw this and challenged Moses. He said the workload was too heavy, preventing Moses from working wisely and wearing both Moses and the people out (imagine waiting for your turn in court in a single line with thousands of others). Jethro told Moses how to delegate the work to satisfy the people and relieve the personal strain, freeing Moses to lead wisely.

To keep improving our leadership, we must continually discern between mere activity and actual accomplishment. Doing the wrong things well thwarts many would-be leaders. Take out your calendar, your to-do lists, and your reflections of the last few days. What is stealing your time? What needs to be on your stop-doing list?

LEAVING A LEGACY

There is no remembrance of men of old, and even those who are yet to come will not be remembered by those who follow.

Ecclesiastes 1:11

What really ignites your passion? What keeps you up at night? Is it your desire to make a difference? Is it your hope to leave a legacy? We love thinking big. We love to look years ahead at what we hope to build, what we'll be remembered for. But Solomon says, "You're mistaken. You're only dreaming. What you do won't matter."

Solomon is really referring to the audacious, noble, well-intended, prideful goals that we think WE can accomplish. He is suggesting that you and I, like him, think far too highly of ourselves, that we give ourselves far more credit than we deserve, and we over-estimate our contributions to our communities.

Our giftedness, strategic thinking, education, experience, influence, passion, hard work, commitment, and win-loss records will all be eventually forgotten apart from how God chooses to use us. God is looking to shape history with humble people with a spirit of dependence and a subjection to his authority. Just look at Abraham, Moses, Gideon, David, or the twelve disciples. They were "nobodies" in terms of nobility, appearance, and abilities, but God loved their hearts and used them to shape history. God would rather use a humble nobody than a prideful "ten-talent" guy to make a lasting impression.

When you bring humility and obedience to the game, God shapes you to shape history. When you don't, little else matters.

GENUINE PRAYERS

Your Father knows what you need before you ask him.

Matthew 6:8

Most of us have neutered our prayers. We've been taught to pray politely and respectfully, perhaps even rhythmically. God seems to want something more genuine. He wants our words to him to reflect our true feelings. He yearns for our prayers to resemble our conversations with our best friends rather than our prepared statements to the administration or the press.

Have you ever really "taken off the gloves" and expressed your most painful feelings and questions to God in prayer? He already knows what you're going through. He knows what you're thinking. Sharing anything short of your real feelings must seem awfully shallow or phony to the God who already knows your heart.

LISTENING AND LEARNING

Let the wise listen and add to their learning, and let the discerning get guidance.

Proverbs 1:5

Ever notice how many young leaders have early success and then just seem to fade away? One of the trappings of success is reading and believing the headlines about ourselves. When we think we've arrived, we tend to stop listening and learning.

Biologists tell us that every living organism is either growing or dying. Leaders who lack intentional exposure to new thoughts and challenges may feel good about themselves, but make no mistake—their leadership is dying. Are you committed to personal and professional growth? What have you done in the last sixty days to stretch yourself? If you continue learning at your current pace, where will you be a year from now?

KNOWN BY OUR ACTIONS

Even a child is known by his actions, by whether his conduct is pure and right.

Proverbs 20:11

I know it's cliché, but actions speak louder than words. What we do says far more about us than what we say. It's easy to quote Bible verses and season our conversations with religious language. We think we're letting our light shine by offering to pray for a team member going through tough times. But what happens five minutes later when that same team member watches us cuss another out for "dropping the ball"? What are we telling those we have been entrusted to lead about Christianity when we lead devotions, and then they hear us lie and gossip?

Don't kid yourself. People watch Christians in leadership. They may not say anything when your actions align with your words. But they definitely notice when your actions deviate from what you claim.

God does not expect perfection. No one is perfect. But you don't want your carelessness to come between someone else and God. Don't let your mouth or your careless actions undermine your opportunity to make a Kingdom impact.

WORTHY WORDS AND ACTIONS

Whatever happens, conduct yourselves in a manner worthy of the gospel of Christ.

Philippians 1:27

Some leaders struggle with this calling just before closing a big deal, when the pressure is growing. Some leaders struggle with acting and speaking dishonorably in the heat of the moment when a deal is on the line. Some tend to fall short while celebrating a big win, while others find this calling hardest after an unexpected loss.

Our Lord did not suffer a gruesome death for net profits. He gave his life so that we might live. He deserves our gratitude. He deserves our love. He deserves our respect and obedience. If we believe in his omnipresence, if we believe he is near at all times, if we believe he hears our every word and sees our every deed, if we have been entrusted to lead, how do we justify continually dishonoring him before others?

Leadership is about more than business. Leadership shapes lives. The words and actions you choose speak volumes into the lives of those you influence. James says teachers will be judged more strictly than others. It is hard to imagine a leader who is not a teacher.

James also says that a salt spring cannot produce fresh water. In other words, your words and actions are indicators of your heart. You may have the resumé and the experience, but if your heart is not prepared for leadership, you will dishonor Christ through leading. What are you doing to prepare your heart for leadership? Are you investing time with God and in his Word?

YOUR TEAM'S
SWEET SPOT

So the Twelve gathered all the disciples together and said, "It would not be right for us to neglect the ministry of the word of God in order to wait on tables...

We will turn this responsibility over to them and will give our attention to prayer and the ministry of the word."

Acts 6:2, 3b, 4

What do you do well? What else are you doing? What are your team members doing? Are you holding onto responsibilities simply because you want them done right? The best teams are always built around strengths, passions, and needs. Pride and fear keep us from developing people around us and delegating responsibilities.

Your team's sweet spot will be found when each person finds the intersection of his strengths and passions and the team's needs. You know the needs. Do you know each person well enough to know their strengths and passions? Do you have the humility and courage to do so?

THE SIZE OF THE FIGHT IN THE DOG

We are therefore Christ's ambassadors, as though God were making his appeal through us.

2 Corinthians 5:20

There are approximately 155 million regular churchgoers in America. In other words, we have enough team members to have a much greater kingdom impact. Stop for a moment and let that sink in. Imagine the possibilities if every churchgoer took the call to be an ambassador for Christ seriously. As the old saying goes, "it is not the size of the dog in the fight, but the size of the fight in the dog" that matters.

The moral fabric of our nation is unraveling. We are increasingly and openly embracing unprecedented levels of sin, corruption, greed, and deceit. Unfortunately, each new generation will accept this tide of ungodliness as normal, *unless* trusted Christian leaders take their calling seriously and un-ashamedly, consistently honor their Lord and Savior.

God can choose to change the direction of our nation. But he has been clear that he will only do so through humble, godly leaders stepping forward and taking a stand. Who is in a better position to model godly leadership than workplace leaders? You have been chosen for leadership. You have your team members' undivided attention. You have responsibilities for the largest block of waking hours each day for each of them. You have opportunities to make a difference. You're already a "big dog." The question is "the size of the fight in the dog." As many have discovered, being an ambassador for Christ may not be an easy, convenient, politically-correct, or even socially acceptable calling. Surely, you won't call yourself a leader *and* a Christian and simply stay on the porch.

STAND FIRM

Therefore, my dear brothers, stand firm. Let nothing move you. Always give yourselves fully to the work of the Lord, because you know that your labor in the Lord is not in vain.

1 Corinthians 15:58

Some times are just plain tough. There are days when each of us just wants to throw in the towel, wondering why we do what we do. Those are the days when the evil one begins to whisper words of self-doubt and despair. He wants us to think our work is in vain. He wants us to think we don't make a difference. He points to our team members who have embarrassed, disgraced, or worse. He points to the betrayals of others. He highlights our mistakes and shortcomings. He speaks through others both from afar and from within our inner circles. But the most dangerous voice is the one in our own heads: "This is a waste." "I am wasting my life." "This doesn't matter." "The guys who cut corners always end up on top." "The whole world is against me."

You and I have been called to be obedient to the gospel, to follow Jesus, to be indwelt, empowered, and led by the Holy Spirit. We are called to honor the name of Jesus through our lives. What we do in the Lord is not in vain. We are not building a house simply to blow it up. We are not writing a paper simply to delete it. We are not making furniture simply to throw it in the fire. Leadership is a noble calling. You have been entrusted to shape the lives of those you lead. In positively influencing their lives, you are shaping the future of your community, our society, the church, and the kingdom. Scripture tells us that Jesus will complete what we have started in his name when he returns.

Your work matters to God. He is watching. Let him lead you. Let him empower you. When you honor him in the smallest of ways, you're building the kingdom. He will complete your work. He planted you right where you are. Stand firm. You matter.

WISDOM IS SUPREME

Wisdom is supreme; therefore get wisdom. Though it cost all you have, get understanding. Esteem her, and she will exalt you; embrace her, and she will honor you.

Proverbs 4:7-8

Wisdom is God's perspective. It is seeing my circumstances, the people around me, my expectations, and the expectations of others as God sees them. For the leader who wishes to honor God, wisdom is without comparison. Solomon, whom the Bible says was the wisest man who ever lived, says "wisdom is supreme."

We gain wisdom through hearing, reading, and studying the Word of God. We also gain wisdom by seeking wise counsel and accountability from others committed to honoring God. During peak season, some leaders decide that they are too busy to participate in such endeavors. We seem to run out of time and/or energy to read Scripture daily, make church on Sunday, go to Bible study, or continue meeting with a trusted advisor.

Imagine a welder who wears his face shield until it's time to make a weld, a police officer who takes off his Kevlar vest to answer a domestic response, or a nurse who removes her glasses before drawing blood. If these examples seem silly, consider the leader who stops seeking wisdom when he needs it most.

The God who called you to lead will not abandon you. Why would you even consider abandoning him when you need him most? Lean into the Word and gain a clearer, more accurate perspective of the chaos around you, as well as a deeper sense of peace within you.

POSING

Simply let your "yes" be "yes" and your "no," "no"; anything beyond this comes from the evil one.

Matthew 5:37

The workplace is full of posers. You know the type: boasting what they don't intend to deliver; covering up their own liability to avoid consequences; misleading staff to think a promotion, a raise, or restructuring is closer than it is; offering excuses to hide reality; manipulating numbers to paint a favorable picture; omitting facts that reveal reality; misrepresenting experience.

Jesus reserved his harshest criticism for the posers of his day, the Pharisees, those leaders who claimed to be godly, but instead simply posed. Your ability to shape the lives of those you have been entrusted to lead will be directly proportional to your ability to be real with other people.

Playing the political game, straddling the fence, and telling people what you think they want to hear are just forms of posing. Jesus says soft, wishy-washy answers are from the evil one, and they eventually bring bitterness and resentment. Don't fall into this trap! If you cannot answer "yes" or "no," simply ask for time to think and pray about the issue and don't answer until your yes is yes or your no is no.

KICKING BACK

Come to me, all you who are weary and burdened, and I will give you rest. Take my yoke upon you and learn from me, for I am gentle and humble in heart, and you will find rest for your souls.

Matthew 11:28-29

Workplace leadership is a demanding responsibility. It's easy to feel pressured into working sixty to seventy hours per week. You address countless disputes, fret over difficult decisions, face unanswerable questions, eat unforgiving meals, and often lie awake in the middle of the night just staring at the ceiling.

Christianity is not about adding to that burden. Jesus does not want you to read his Word and speak to him out of obligation. He wants you to know him and enjoy his presence like a great cup of coffee, a well-worn jersey, your favorite fishing hole, or an ultra-smooth transmission. He prepared for each day with a quiet conversation with his dad, and he eagerly welcomes you to join them.

Jesus actually promises to give us rest when we set aside our formal pretensions, take a deep breath, exhale, and chill with him. Your daily personal quiet time should be less about checklists and more about kicking back and learning from the guy who turned water to wine and cooked breakfast on the beach.

TELL GREAT STORIES

So Jesus called them and spoke to them in parables.

Mark 3:23

Jesus, the greatest leader of all time, did not just happen to tell stories. He could have mastered any form of communication, and he chose to tell stories. Why? Everyone loves a good story.

Great leaders know the power of great stories. Great stories are inspiring and challenging. They are entertaining while making important, relevant points. We remember and understand Jesus' teaching on compassion, generosity, and restoration because of the stories he told about the Good Samaritan, the poor widow, and the prodigal son. Like Jesus, wise leaders share great stories that create heroes, develop legends, and serve to establish the kind of expectant culture that inspires their athletes to greatness. Of course, the greatest stories are those of God's greatness, strength, grace, goodness, mercy, and love found in the pages of your Bible. When is the last time you shared one of the greatest stories of all time to inspire your team?

POOR PERFORMERS

But Paul did not think it wise to take him, because he had deserted them in Pamphylia and had not continued with them in the work.

Acts 15:38

Some of a leader's toughest decisions concern responding to poor performers. Consider the following steps when doing so:

PRAY—Ask God to give you his perspective on the performance and person.

Explore the 3Cs:

1. Is this a character issue?

2. Is this a competency issue?

3. Is this a chemistry issue?

Does this person *clearly understand* the roles, goals, responsibilities, and standards for this position?

Why is this person under-performing? Is it a lack of:

- training?
- motivation?
- experience?
- ability?
- clear assignment?

Consider your perspective. Instead of the old "I need to get rid of this person" mentality, consider this: Several biblical writers tell us that life is short. James says life is "but a vapor." When you appropriately release a person from a position in which he is failing, you are releasing him from that failure and freeing him to seek a role in which he can find success. Too many people are wasting their short lives in unfulfilling and unproductive jobs. With a proper release, it's even possible to instill in the person the excitement that comes from anticipating a new venture. It's not that this process will become easy. But the right perspective is one of releasing a person from failure to pursue something more fulfilling.

WHEN WORDS
ARE MANY

When words are many, sin is not absent, but he who holds his tongue is wise.

Proverbs 10:19

Think of a situation that you vowed never to repeat. We all have them. Chances are that either someone spoke far too much, or perhaps it was a simple look from the right person that communicated far more than words ever could.

Fools love to hear themselves talk. People who consider themselves above and beyond those listening also love to hear themselves talk. But where there is mutual respect, fewer words are needed, especially when facing a challenge. Compare the offices of a below- average-performing small business to the offices of a high-performing small business. The former is almost certain to have teammates vying for attention, while mutual respect for people and ideas fill the latter.

What I have learned through observation is that the level of unproductive and inappropriate chatter from the team members is usually indicative of the level of chatter and respect among leaders. The more self-centered and disrespectful the leaders, the more self-centered and disrespectful the team members tend to be. Are you setting the example you wish your team to follow? Are you choosing your words carefully?

GOD'S CHARACTER

But the fruit of the Spirit is love, joy, peace, patience, kindness, goodness, faithfulness, gentleness, and self-control.

Galatians 5:22

Ever wrestle with the characteristics listed in Galatians 5:22? They are the personal characteristics of God. The Holy Spirit is the invisible presence of God dwelling within every believer. If you have the Holy Spirit within you, which the Bible says every believer does, then you already have all of his characteristics within you. No one gets a partial dose.

The way to exhibit more peace, patience, or self-control is not to work harder at doing so. The Holy Spirit, living within you, already has these characteristics. If you want to exhibit more of God's character in and through your life, stop trying to manufacture the appearance and spend more time with the God you hope to reflect. The more you trust and submit to him, the more he will be seen in and through your life.

FRESH BAKED COOKIES

Taste and see that the Lord is good...

Psalm 34:8

How did you approach this devotion? With enthusiasm, or out of a sense of obligation? How do you usually approach worship? Reading Scripture? Prayer?

We are among the busiest people in the history of the world. Few of us can function without some form of to-do lists, and most of us simply layer to-do lists over one another. We have to-do lists with personal necessities, then we add a layer of to-do lists with family or household needs, then we add layers for professional obligations, ministry commitments, and community expectations. Finally, we add a layer for matters of faith.

Jesus does not want to be approached as an obligation. He puts little value in checking Bible study, quiet time, church attendance, or prayer off your list. While these are great endeavors, they are meant to help us know him better. Apart from knowing him better, our religious checklists are meaningless and counterproductive. Jesus wants a relationship with you. He wants his presence to be eagerly anticipated and celebrated, not simply considered or pondered. He wants to be approached less out of obligation and more like we'd approach a plate of fresh-baked cookies, brick-oven pizza, or a thick, juicy ribeye.

IS IT BENEFICIAL?
IS IT BINDING?

Everything is permissible for me—but not everything is beneficial. Everything is permissible for me—but I will not be mastered by anything.

1 Corinthians 6:12

There are far too many people fighting for "rights" without considering what is beneficial or binding. Only a fool will pursue that which is not beneficial or that which will bind or master him simply because he has the right to do so. Too many of us engage in activities which threaten to steal our influence, our careers, our marriages, or even our health, and yet we argue that it is our "right" to do so. We line up to exchange long-term peace and freedom for short-term pleasure.

God loves us. He wants us to experience peace and freedom. The Apostle Paul says that while we may have a legal right or it may be socially acceptable, we should remember that "You are not your own; you were bought at a price." To overlook what Jesus has done for us by engaging in that which will take our peace and freedom is foolishness.

WHITE LIES

Do not lie to each other, since you have taken off your old self with its practices and have put on the new self, which is being renewed in knowledge in the image of its creator.

Colossians 3:9-10

I suppose some of you may feel belittled if I simply told you to tell the truth. Every person reading this knows the potential consequences of lying. But what about *white lies*? What about those times when we tell an assistant to tell someone we've left for the day to avoid a long, untimely conversation? Or when we tell a customer we'll meet their deadline when we know we can't quite make it? Or when we suggest that we never received an e-mail that made an inconvenient request?

The Oxford Dictionary defines a *white lie* as "a harmless or trivial untruth." Most of us want to distinguish between our own white lies and "whoppers." But how does the Bible tell us to distinguish the difference? The Bible says there is no difference. In fact, the Bible warns us about categorizing or prioritizing sin of any kind. The Bible says there is no "trivial or harmless untruth." A lie is a lie.

As a leader, you must recognize that people are watching and remembering far more about you than you realize. The integrity of your organization will never exceed the integrity of your leadership. Each time your team members hear you lie, they understand that lying is acceptable in your organization in certain circumstances. At that point, they will use their own judgment, not yours, about which circumstances justify lying.

ARE YOU LISTENING?

He who answers before listening–that is his folly and his shame.

Proverbs 18:13

A fool finds no pleasure in understanding but delights in airing his own opinions.

Proverbs 18:2

Most leaders invest vast amounts of energy developing their own skills, such as long-term planning, cold-calling, recognizing the competition's strategic moves, prioritizing responsibilities, delegation, time-management, and public speaking. But sometimes, we think experience neutralizes our need to listen. We've been here, done that, got the t-shirt.

The Bible says that's just a foolish attitude. You and I will always learn more by listening than speaking. We never outgrow the need to grow, and one of the most vital means of growth is listening. The most humbling experiences often follow those times when we think we have all the answers. Perhaps it's time to admit we neither have all the answers nor all the questions. Great ideas can come from the most unlikely of sources, if we're open to listening. Are *you* listening?

SELECTING LEADERS

The Lord does not look at the things man looks at. Man looks at the outward appearance, but the Lord looks at the heart.

1 Samuel 16:7

When sent to find the new king of Israel, Samuel first looked at the sons of Jesse just like everyone else did–from man's perspective. He expected to see the anointing of God through man's measurements. But God looks beyond physical size, talent, appearance, gifts, intellect, speed, strength, and everything else to peer into a man's heart.

When selecting leaders, we are always wise to follow God's approach. God always selects a person of character for leadership. Humility, obedience, and submission to God's authority are the cornerstones to God's selection process.

Popular opinion is irrelevant to God. He often sidelines those expected to succeed and does the extraordinary through the most ordinary of leaders because he is looking beyond outward appearances into the heart. Do you know your leaders well enough to know their hearts? Are you keeping those who have compromised their character in leadership roles for the wrong reasons? Compromised character leads to a compromised team.

TRIPPING A TEAMMATE

Be careful, however, that the exercise of your freedom does not become a stumbling block to the weak.

1 Corinthians 8:9

What is your personal vice? What's that one thing that you know some people object to you doing, but you do it anyway? Maybe it's drinking—but you're over —twenty-one. Maybe it's tobacco—it's your right to choose. Perhaps it's profanity—get over it.

Your vice is most likely legal, not prohibited in Scripture, and perhaps widely accepted among your friends and peers. But what about weaker, impressionable, or immature people who look to you as a Christian leader? Like it or not, leaders are in the business of influencing behavior. If you're somewhere people recognize you as a leader, you're still influencing behavior. You may enjoy your vice, but does it align with the influence you hope to have and the legacy you hope to leave? We will each be held accountable for how we steward the opportunities given us. No one wants to be remembered for tripping a teammate.

SUCCESS

Still other seed fell on good soil.

Mark 4:8

In business, results matter. Effort is important and often, but not always, leads to profits. But at the end of the project, it is the bottom line, not the effort, which will determine if you succeed or not. Every workplace leader knows and appreciates this. Those who think great efforts are enough eventually find themselves looking for another profession.

Yet, even the best leaders realize that it is impossible to always succeed. Leaders who cannot handle defeat and rejection don't last long. Leaders must believe that if they put forth the right effort, success will come.

Sometimes we simply use the wrong metrics. We see others leading people to confess Christ just as some of our own seem to reject everything we stand for. We get word that a team member is in jail, and we just want to go into a cave. In Mark 4, Jesus tells the story of the sower. The sower could not know in advance where to find the best soil, so he broadcast the seed in all directions.

As a leader, you may extend a helping hand to a family, share your testimony, pray with a co-worker, find a way to serve your community, host a weekly devotion or Bible study, boldly pray before or after each meeting, or quietly pray for your team. The story seems to indicate that the sower was responsible for making the effort while the score, 1–3, was immaterial. When it comes to eternal matters, you will never be held accountable for the responses of others. But you are accountable for making an effort. Sometimes success simply means sowing.

RESPONDING TO MOCKERS

Whoever corrects a mocker invites insult; whoever rebukes a wicked man incurs abuse. Do not rebuke a mocker or he will hate you; rebuke a wise man and he will love you. Instruct a wise man and he will be wiser still; teach a righteous man and he will add to his learning.

Proverbs 9:7-9

In Proverbs, "mockers" are characterized by an unwillingness to address character issues. Inevitably, this unwillingness leads to destructive behaviors. The question for leaders becomes—"What do we expect of these mockers?" Apart from a relational encounter with Jesus Christ, mockers will consistently act in line with their character—or lack thereof. Proverbs says that to expect otherwise is simply foolishness.

On the other hand, when we correct or challenge someone we have been entrusted to lead, and they respond with gratitude and show us a genuine effort to address personal character issues, we should pour ourselves into them.

Far too many leaders invest far too much time in chasing talented, immoral, corrupt prima donnas simply because they have a skill set we want. Leaders who compromise their integrity for flashy, ungrateful "players," while neglecting the long-term opportunities with others eager to grow, find themselves insulted, used-up, and worn-out.

YOUR GAME PLAN

> *Therefore go and make disciples of all nations, baptizing them in the name of the Father and of the Son and of the Holy Spirit, and teaching them to obey everything I have commanded you. And surely I am with you always, to the very end of the age.*
>
> **Matthew 28:19-20**

Jesus had a clear understanding about what mattered most, what he expected of his team, what they would need, and how they were doing. He also clearly communicated and reinforced each expectation.

Great leaders understand the need to know and communicate what matters most, what they expect of their team, what they will need, and how they are doing. Paul "Bear" Bryant, the legendary Alabama football coach, had five points that explained what he believed a coach should do:

- Tell players what you expect of them.

- Give players an opportunity to perform.

- Let players know how they are getting along.

- Instruct and empower players when they need it.

- Reward players according to their contributions.

What's your game plan? What matters most? What do you expect of each team member? What will they need? How are they doing? Have you communicated each of these to each of them?

TRADING UP

The kingdom of heaven is like a merchant looking for fine pearls. When he found one of great value, he went away and sold everything he had and bought it.

Matthew 13:45-46

You think you know what you want and where you want to be. But are you willing to pay the price? It takes passion to keep growing, learning, and trading up. One can only make a successful trade when one has something of value to exchange. Most unsuccessful leaders have not worked to develop anything worth trading. They have failed to invest their time and energies wisely. They feel "stuck" in their frustration. They may have always dreamed of leading, but they have not put in the effort to succeed once they "got in the game."

Many Christians face a similar frustration. They have received salvation. Yet they struggle with anxiety, bitterness, pride, discontent, a lack of self-control, or impatience. They feel stuck in their frustration. They are missing the opportunities for love, peace, joy, and fulfillment before them because they have failed to invest their time and energy into a relationship with God. We trade up our lives and our impact by prioritizing time with God.

Are you as fruitful and fulfilled as you want to be? If not, what could you do to change that? Are you willing to do so?

NOTHING IS IMPOSSIBLE

I can do all things through him who strengthens me.

Philippians 4:13

Nothing is impossible for the God who spoke the world into existence. Which of your concerns might overwhelm the God who parted the Red Sea, healed the sick, gave sight to the blind, raised the dead, cast out demons, could not be tempted, and overcame death?

Comparing his strength to ours is like comparing a locomotive to a microbe; His power, like comparing a nuclear reactor to a firefly.

And Paul says his power strengthens us. Who could stand against us? When we stop treating him like a flash light, a genie in a bottle, or a pharmacist filling our prescription, and trust him to provide exactly what we need, nothing is impossible. Just read the stories of Moses, Noah, Elijah, David, Joseph, and Peter.

LIGHT

I am the light of the world. Whoever follows me will never walk in darkness, but will have the light of life.

John 8:12

I found the following definitions regarding properties of objects interacting with light on my daughter's science homework:

Opaque—No visible light passes through. No image can be seen.

Translucent—Some light passes through, but the material distorts the image.

Transparent—Most light passes through, allowing a clear image to be seen.

My mind immediately went to my willingness to allow Christ to be seen through me in my everyday interactions.

When you consider Jesus as the light of the world, which of the three properties best describes you today? What if we asked your team members? Your co-workers? Your family? Your friends?

THE LION'S ROAR

A king's rage is like the roar of a lion, but his favor is like dew on the grass.

Proverbs 19:12

Some leaders seem to think it's all about them. Everything revolves around their own records, goals, and desires. Their idea of a team is a collection of people doing whatever they tell them to do. Just step back, listening to them rant and rave, and you might just see some similarities between them and a naturally self-centered two-year-old.

The lion's roar is one of the most fearsome sounds in all of nature. But, as awesome as a lion's roar is, it would become commonplace, losing its impact, if it was heard throughout each day. A wise leader knows that consistent encouragement is needed to temper and balance his roar in order to cultivate unity, trust, stability, passion, hope, competence, clarity, and discipline.

For more information about
John Crosby
&
Called to Lead
please visit:

www.priorityinsight.com
john@priorityinsight.com
www.facebook.com/PriorityInsight

For more information about
AMBASSADOR INTERNATIONAL
please visit:

www.ambassador-international.com
@AmbassadorIntl
www.facebook.com/AmbassadorIntl